Resources and Techniques for User and Author Profiling in Abusive Language (ResT-UP 2020)

Marseille, France
11 – 16 May 2020

Editors:

Johanna Monti
Valerio Basile
Maria Pia Di Buono
Raffaele Manna
Antonio Pascucci
Sara Tonelli

ISBN: 978-1-7138-1276-0

Printed from e-media with permission by:

Curran Associates, Inc.
57 Morehouse Lane
Red Hook, NY 12571

CURRAN ASSOCIATES INC. proceedings.com

Some format issues inherent in the e-media version may also appear in this print version.

Association for Computational Linguistics
209 N. Eighth Street
Stroudsburg, Pennsylvania 18360

Phone: 1-570-476-8006
Fax: 1-570-476-0860

acl@aclweb.org

Additional copies of this publication are available from:

Curran Associates, Inc.
57 Morehouse Lane
Red Hook, NY 12571 USA
Phone: 845-758-0400
Fax: 845-758-2633
Email: curran@proceedings.com
Web: www.proceedings.com

LREC 2020 Workshop
Language Resources and Evaluation Conference
11–16 May 2020

Resources and Techniques for User and Author Profiling in Abusive Language (ResT-UP 2020)

PROCEEDINGS

Editors:
Johanna Monti, Valerio Basile, Maria Pia Di Buono, Raffaele Manna, Antonio Pascucci and Sara Tonelli

Proceedings of the LREC 2020 workshop on Resources and Techniques for User and Author Profiling in Abusive Language (ResT-UP 2020)

Edited by:
Johanna Monti, Valerio Basile, Maria Pia Di Buono, Raffaele Manna, Antonio Pascucci and Sara Tonelli

For more information:
European Language Resources Association (ELRA)
9 rue des Cordelières
75013, Paris
France
http://www.elra.info
Email: lrec@elda.org

Preface by the Workshop Organizers

Welcome to the LREC2020 Workshop on Resources and Techniques for User and Author Profiling in Abusive Language (ResT-UP).

This volume documents the Proceedings of the 1st Workshop on Resources and Techniques for User and Author Profiling in Abusive Language (ResT-UP), held online on 12 May 2020 as part of the LREC 2020 conference (International Conference on Language Resources and Evaluation).
The workshop aimed at bringing together researchers and scholars working on author profiling and automatic detection of abusive language on the Web, e.g., cyberbullying or hate speech, with a twofold objective: improving the existing LRs, e.g., datasets, corpora, lexicons, and sharing ideas on stylometry techniques and features needed for profile information extraction and classification. ResT-UP targeted Profiling scholars and research groups, experts in Statistic and Stylistic Analysis of texts as well as computational linguists who investigate author profile and personality both in short texts (social media posts, blog texts and email) and in long texts (such as pamphlets, (fake) news and political documents). ReST-UP represented an opportunity to share profiling experiments with the scientific community and to show automatic detection techniques of abusive language on the Web. Despite the cancellation of LREC 2020 due to the COVID-19 international emergency, ResT-UP was organized online on Microsoft Teams on May 12th 2020 and the programme included three oral presentations, and featured an invited talk by Paolo Rosso. ResT-UP was attended by about fifty representatives of academic and industrial organisations. We would like to thank the invited speaker, all authors who contributed papers to this workshop edition and the Programme Committee members who provided valuable feedback during the review process.

Johanna Monti – L'Orientale University of Naples – UNIOR NLP Research Group
Valerio Basile – University of Turin
Maria Pia Di Buono – L'Orientale University of Naples – UNIOR NLP Research Group
Raffaele Manna – L'Orientale University of Naples – UNIOR NLP Research Group
Antonio Pascucci – L'Orientale University of Naples – UNIOR NLP Research Group
Sara Tonelli – Fondazione Bruno Kessler, Digital Humanities research group

Organizers

Johanna Monti – L'Orientale University of Naples – UNIOR NLP Research Group
Valerio Basile – University of Turin
Maria Pia Di Buono – L'Orientale University of Naples – UNIOR NLP Research Group
Raffaele Manna – L'Orientale University of Naples – UNIOR NLP Research Group
Antonio Pascucci – L'Orientale University of Naples – UNIOR NLP Research Group
Sara Tonelli – Fondazione Bruno Kessler, Digital Humanities research group

Program Committee:

Cristina Bosco, University of Turin (ITALY)
Tommaso Caselli, University of Groningen (NETHERLANDS)
Walter Daelemans, University of Antwerp (BELGIUM)
Rossana Damiano, University of Turin (ITALY)
Maciej Eder, Pedagogical University of Kraków (POLAND)
Francesca Frontini, Université Paul Valéry Montpellier 3 (FRANCE)
Dimitrios Kokkinakis, University of Göteborg (SWEDEN)
Stefano Menini, Fondazione Bruno Kessler (ITALY)
Cataldo Musto, University of Bari (ITALY)
Malvina Nissim, University of Groningen (NETHERLANDS)
Michael Oakes, University of Wolverhampton (UNITED KINGDOM)
Alessio Palmero Aprosio, Fondazione Bruno Kessler (ITALY)
Viviana Patti, University of Turin (ITALY)
Marco Polignano, University of Bari (ITALY)
Paolo Rosso, Universitat Politècnica de València (SPAIN)
Manuela Sanguinetti, University of Turin (ITALY)
Efstathios Stamatatos, University of Aegean (GREECE)
Natalia Viani, King's College London (UNITED KINGDOM)
Marcos Zampieri, Rochester Institute of Technology (U.S.A.)

Invited Speaker:

Paolo Rosso, Universitat Politècnica de València

Prof. Paolo Rosso is Full Professor at the Universitat Politècnica de València, Spain. Prof. Paolo Rosso received his PhD in Computer Science at the Trinity College University of Dublin, Ireland, in 1999. He is member of the Natural Language Engineering Lab. at Pattern Recognition and Human Language Technologies (PRHLT) Research Center. His research focuses on Author Profiling in Social Media, Irony Detection and Opinion Mining, Deceptive Opinion Detection, Stance Detection, Fake News Detection, Hate Speech Detection, Mixed-script Text Analysis and Plagiarism and Social Copying Detection.

Table of Contents

Conference Program

Tuesday 12 May 2020

17:30–18:00 *Profiling Bots, Fake News Spreaders and Haters*
Paolo Rosso

16:30–16:50 *An Indian Language Social Media Collection for Hate and Offensive Speech*
Anita Saroj and Sukomal Pal

16:50–17:10 *Profiling Italian Misogynist: An Empirical Study*
Elisabetta Fersini, Debora Nozza and Giulia Boifava

17:10–17:30 *Lower Bias, Higher Density Abusive Language Datasets: A Recipe*
Juliet van Rosendaal, Tommaso Caselli and Malvina Nissim

Resources and Techniques for User and Author Profiling in Abusive Language (ResT-UP 2020), page 1
Language Resources and Evaluation Conference (LREC 2020), Marseille, 11–16 May 2020

Paolo Rosso, Universitat Politècnica de València

Profiling Bots, Fake News Spreaders and Haters

Author profiling studies how language is shared by people. Stylometry techniques help in identifying aspects such as gender, age, native language, or even personality. Author profiling is a problem of growing importance, not only in marketing and forensics, but also in cybersecurity. The aim is not only to identify users whose messages are potential threats from a terrorism viewpoint but also those whose messages are a threat from a social excusion perspective because containing hate speech, cyberbullying etc.

Bots often play a key role in spreading hate speech, as well as fake news, with the purpose of polarizing the public opinion with respect to controversial issues like Brexit or the Catalan referendum. For instance, the authors of a recent study about the 1 Oct 2017 Catalan referendum, showed that in a dataset with 3.6 million tweets, about 23.6% of tweets were produced by bots. The target of these bots were pro independence influencers that were sent negative, emotional and aggressive hateful tweets with hashtags such as #sonunesbesties (i.e. #theyareanimals).

Since 2013 at the PAN Lab at CLEF (https://pan.webis.de/) we have addressed several aspects of author profiling in social media. In 2019 we investigated the feasibility of distinguishing whether the author of a Twitter feed is a bot, while this year we are addressing the problem of profiling those authors that are more likely to spread fake news in Twitter because they did in the past. We aim at identifying possible fake news spreaders as a first step towards preventing fake news from being propagated among online users (fake news aim to polarize the public opinion and may contain hate speech).

In 2021 we specifically aim at addressing the challenging problem of profiling haters in social media in order to monitor abusive language and prevent cases of social exclusion in order to combat, for instance, racism, xenophobia and misoginy. Although we already started addressing the problem of detecting hate speech when targets are immigrants or women at the HatEval shared task in SemEval-2019, and when targets are women also in the Automatic Misogeny Identification tasks at IberEval-2018, Evalita-2018 and Evalita-2020, it was not done from an author profiling perspective. At the end of the keynote I will present some insights in order to stress the importance of monitoring abusive language in social media, for instance, in foreseeing sexual crimes. In fact, previous studies confirmed that a correlation might lay between the yearly per capita rate of rape and the misogynistic language used in Twitter.

Resources and Techniques for User and Author Profiling in Abusive Language (ResT-UP 2020), pages 2–8
Language Resources and Evaluation Conference (LREC 2020), Marseille, 11–16 May 2020

An Indian Language Social Media Collection for Hate and Offensive Speech

Anita Saroj, Sukomal Pal
Department of Computer Science & Engineering
Indian Institute of Technology (BHU), Varanasi-221005, UP
anitas.rs.cse16@iitbhu.ac.in, spal.cse@iitbhu.ac.in

Abstract

In social media, people express themselves every day on issues that affect their lives. During the parliamentary elections, people's interaction with the candidates in social media posts reflects a lot of social trends in a charged atmosphere. People's likes and dislikes on leaders, political parties and their stands often become subject of hate and offensive posts. We collected social media posts in Hindi and English from Facebook and Twitter during the run-up to the parliamentary election 2019 of India (PEI data-2019). We created a dataset for sentiment analysis into three categories: hate speech, offensive and not hate, or not offensive. We report here the initial results of sentiment classification for the dataset using different classifiers.

Keywords: Twitter, Facebook, parliamentary Election, Hate Speech, Offensive

1. Introduction

Recent years have seen indiscriminate spread of offensive languages on social media platforms such as Facebook and Twitter. Hate speech and offensive posts day by day are growing on social media. People post messages or tweets, often targeting other people with hate and nasty words. Such messages often hurt people, causing at times immense psychological distress and mental trauma to users. Instead of bringing people together, it causes digital divide and social alienation to many. Such practices should be minimized, if can not be stopped entirely for reasons like maintaining the civility and decorum of any forum so that everyone can feel at home to participate. But often absence of any moderator to flag a post objectionable makes the job difficult. Efforts are, therefore, on to automatically detect the use of various forms of abusive languages in social networks, micro-blogs, and blogs so that prevention can also be thought of. Since manual filtering takes a lot of time, and since it can cause symptoms such as post-traumatic stress disorder to human annotators, several research efforts have made to automate this process (Zampieri et al., 2019a).

Few efforts have already been directed to create necessary datasets for automatic identification of offensive languages. The task is formulated as a supervised classification problem, where systems are trained for the presence of some form of abusive or offensive material. **Hate speech** in communication, is deemed to be harmful (individually or at a social level) based on defined 'protected attributes' such as race, disability, sexuality, etc., while **Offensive speech** is simply any communication that upsets someone.

Most of such datasets come from general domain and are in English. In this paper, we focus on in a particular domain with respect to space and time. During any election, when political rivalry reaches the summit, spread and use of obscene language also hit the ceiling. We consider the period of campaigning for general election of India 2019 and interactions of political candidates and people in social media. We present here the first domain-specific data of hate speech and offensive content identification on Parliamentary Election of India 2019 (PEI2019) data for two Languages, English and Hindi. The dataset is created from Twitter and Facebook posts during the Indian Election 2019. It comprises three tasks: a binary classification task, and two multi-class classifications.

Parliamentary Election of India (PEI data) data is especially inspired by two previous evaluation forums: HASOC FIRE 2019 (Mandl et al., 2019a) and SemEval 2019 (Zampieri et al., 2019a), and tries to leverage the synergies of these initiatives. There has been significant work in many languages, particularly for English, and the size of data is large. But there is no domain-specific data of hate speech and offensive content identification- which is the main motivation of making the PEI data. The size of PEI data is small but, we believe, enough to measure the performance of the classification models in Indian language hate speech dataset.

The primary purpose of the paper is to establish a lexical baseline for discriminating between hate speech and offensive speech on domain-specific data. Although some data for hate speech and offensive content identification are available,in English and other languages, there is no such dataset for the Indian language. Here we present a dataset of the Indian language, which is in Hindi and English dataset. We compare PEI 2019 data with two other datasets:

SemEval-2019 Task 6 and FIRE 2019 HASOC dataset.

The rest of the paper is organised as follows. In Sec 2., we do literature survey. Next, we describe the dataset in Sec 3.. We discuss the result in Sec 4.. Finally we conclude in Sec 6.

2. Related Work

Over the last few years, a few studies on hate speech and offensive content identification have been published. Different hate speech and offensive language identification problems are explored in the literature ranging from hate speech, offensive language, bullying content, and aggressive content. Below we discuss some of related works briefly.

2.1. Hate speech identification

Hate speech is a statement of intention to offend another and use harsh or offensive language based on actual or perceived membership to another group (Britannica, 2015). Malmasi and Zampieri (2017) adopted a linear support vector classifier with three groups of extracted features for these tests: word skip-grams, surface n-gram, and Brown cluster. They reported accuracy scores and established a lexical baseline for discriminating between profane and hate speech on the standard dataset (Malmasi and Zampieri, 2017).

2.2. Offensive language identification

While hate speech is targeted to a group of people based on their religion, caste, race, ethnicity or belief, offensive language such as insulting, harmful, derogatory, or obscene material is directed from one person to another and is open to others. Offensive language may be targeted or un-targeted. User-generated content on social media platforms such as Twitter often holds a high level of rough, harmful, or sometimes offensive language (Zampieri et al., 2019b). Increasing vulgarity in online conversations and user commentary have emerged as relevant issues in society as well as in science (Ramakrishnan et al., 2019). identified offensive tweets with an accuracy of 83.14 %, F_1-score 0.7565 on the real test data for the classification of offensive vs non-offensive.

The above tasks are related to that of cyber-bullying and aggressive contents and often differences are blurred. A post can contain one or many of the features above and can belong to many categories. However, we focused here on hate speech and offensive language identification tasks. The datasets mentioned were mostly in English and not domain-specific, but from general domain. As far as language specific collection is concerned, there has been probably the first task as HaSpeeDe 2018 [1] for Italian, PolEval 2019 and 2020 for Polish [2] and SemEval 2019 Task 5 that were domain-specific yet multi-lingual [3]. Here we build a domain-specific collection (political posts during election campaigns), and contain both English and Hindi posts. The vitriolic attacks become fierce as the campaign heats up and use of offensive languages nosedives to its nadir. We would like to see how the task of identifying hate and offensive language in such a collection and to gauge the extent of abusiveness in charged atmosphere.

3. Datasets

In India, the last parliamentary election was held from 11 April to 19 May 2019. During this event, we collected tweets and Facebook messages from social media in two languages Hindi and English. The data is used for training and testing in both hate speech and offensive language identification tasks. PEI data was annotated using a hierarchical three-level annotation model introduced in Zampieri et al. (2019) and Mandl et al. (2019).

3.1. Data Collection

We collected data from Facebook and Twitter during the parliamentary election 2019 of India. For Twitter, the data collection was done using the Twitter API with a tweepy Python library. The tweets collected from elected candidates' Twitter accounts and also collected with keywords #Twitter accounts name' and #Loksabha election, #election 2019, #loksabha election 2019 of India. For the hashtags, the tweets were between 11 April to 23 May 2019. For Facebook, we used the Facepager tool (Dr. Jakob Jünger, 2019) to capture messages. The collected tweets were in English, Hindi, and some other regional languages. For this study, we concentrated on tweets and messages in Hindi and English language. We collected more than ten thousand posts from Facebook and Twitter. Out of them, we found 20% tweets belonging to the hate speech and offensive content. Table 3.1. and Table 3.1. show some example of hate speech and offensive content in English and Hindi respectively.

3.2. Task Description

The dataset is created from Twitter and Facebook and distributed in a tab-separated format. The size of the data corpus is nearly 2000 posts for both English and Hindi separately. Figure 1 shows the categories of the post into different classes. The first stage categorization is Task A, and the second stage is Task B, and then, Task C as defined below.

- **Task A:** We focus on Hate speech and Offensive language identification for Hindi and English during the parliamentary election 2019 in India. Task A is a coarse-grained binary classification in which posts classify into two classes, namely: Hate

[1] http://www.di.unito.it/~tutreeb/haspeede-evalita18/index.html

[2] http://poleval.pl/

[3] https://www.aclweb.org/anthology/S19-2007/

Table 1: Tweets or Facebook messages from the PEI dataset, with their labels for each level of the annotation model of English.

Post	Label		
The Prime Minister talks about economic growth &progress. At the same time his colleagues talk about sending Bollywood stars to Pakistan!	NOT	-	-
NDTV features the Prime Minister's new improved BJP dream team for Karnataka. FRESH out of jail, MODI-FIED and REDDY to steal. #ReddyStingBJPExposed	HOF	HATE	UNT
West Bengal Chief Minister and Trinamool Congress supremo Mamata Banerjee on Monday called Prime Minister Narendra Modi the greatest danger for the country and said she will give her life to ensure that no riot takes place in the state.	HOF	OFFN	TIN

and Offensive (HOF) and Non- Hate, or offensive (NOT).

- **Task B:** This is a fine-grained classification of Task A. Hate-speech and offensive posts from Task A further classified into three categories. **HATE** contains Hate speech content and **OFFN** contain offensive material and **NONE** not hate speech or not offensive.
- **Task C:** This one checks the type of offensive content. Only posts labeled as HOF in Task A are considered here. **Targeted Insult (TIN)** posts hold an abuse/threat to a person, group, or others. **Untargeted (UNT)** posts contain untargeted hate speech and offensive. Posts with general obscenity are considered not targeted, although they contain non-acceptable language.

3.3. Annotation

The annotation is done by three undergraduate students of Engineering whose first language is Hindi for speaking and writing, and they can speak and write English as well. The average score of inter-annotation agreement (Cohen's Kappa) for Task A is 0.87 for the English language and 0.89 for the Hindi language. Similarly, the average Cohen's Kappa for Task B and Task C are 0.85 and 0.89, respectively. We also evaluate Krippendorff's alpha which are 0.90, and 0.89 for English and Hindi respectively. Annotation labels for English and Hindi are shown in Table 1 and Table 2 and Figure 1 shows the hierarchy of annotations.

Table 2: Tweets or Facebook messages from the PEI dataset, with their labels for each level of the annotation model of Hindi.

Post	Label		
आज केरल और वायनाड के किसानों की समस्या लोक-सभा मे उठाया। उम्मीद है सर-कार इनका हल जल्द करेगी। Today the problem of farmers of Kerala and Wayanad was raised in the Lok Sabha. Hope the government solves these.	NOT	-	-
BJP और RSS के लोग धर्म की दलाली करते हैं।इनको न गाय से प्यार है, न धर्म से, इनको सिर्फ सत्ता से प्यार है-कानपुर देहात. People of BJP and RSS broke religion. They neither love cow nor religion, they only love power - Kanpur countryside.	HOF	HATE	TIN
बीजेपी की विचारधारा देश को बांटने की है, दलितों को कु-चलने की है, आदिवासियों को कुचलने की है, अल्पसंख्यकों को कुचलने की है, बीजेपी की उस विचारधारा के खिलाफ हम यहाँ खड़े ह The ideology of the BJP is to divide the country, crush the Dalits, crush the tribals, crush the minorities and are against that ideology of the BJP.	HOF	OFFN	TIN

3.4. Data Summary

We consider Hindi and English language posts for hate speech and offensive content identification and some regional language. English and Hindi are the third and fourth most-spoken languages respectively, with Hindi having the largest number native-speakers in India [4]. Most of our collected posts in Hindi language, and some posts are code-mixed. The data can be used for multiple tasks in multi-way classification.

[4]https://en.wikipedia.org/wiki/Hindi

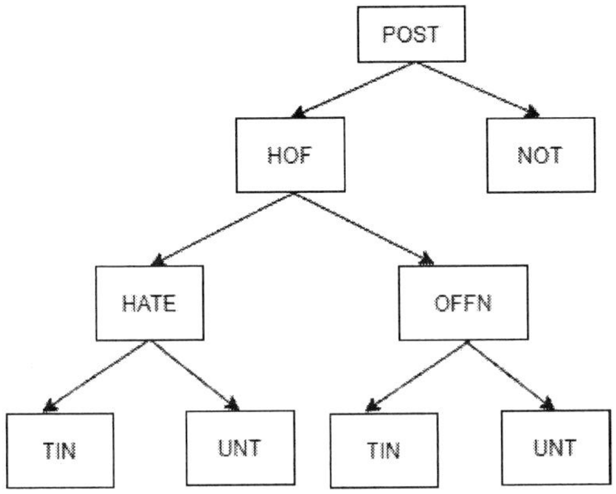

Figure 1: Process of the post or tweet annotation

Table 3: Distribution of labels combinations in PEI data.

Tasks	Labels			Total-Post	
Task A	HOF	NOT	-	Train	Test
Task B	HATE	OFFN	NONE	1519	488
Task C	UNT	TNT	NONE		

3.5. Data Preprocessing

Collected posts are first cleaned using the tweet preprocessing library[5] and several symbols like the Retweets (RT), Hashtags, URLs, Twitter Mentions, Emoji's and Smileys are removed. This pre-processed data also excludes the English stopwords (available in NLTK[6]) while tokenizing the sentences for the extraction of frequency-based feature extraction. Stopword removal and stemming are done on the terms. For prediction, the terms are represented by their tf-idf features considering each post as a document. These represented features are language independent and used for both Hindi and English. We did not use lemmatization, and any other lexical features that are language dependents.

3.6. Classifier

We use four machine learning classifiers: Multinomial Naive-Bayes (MNB), Stochastic Gradient Descent (SGD), Linear Support Vector Machine (Linear SVM), and Linear Regression (LR) for classification of Hate speech and Offensive content. The input for all the classifiers is in the form of tf-idf feature matrix, and output is a label for the categorical result. All the classifiers give different scores, as classifiers have different specialties.

3.7. Existing Data

For comparison, we also use similar data taken from other tasks. The first dataset of hate speech and offensive content is created by Davidson et al. (2017) and the second dataset is created by the HASOC track (FIRE 2019) (Mandl et al., 2019b). The SemEval-2019 Task 6 dataset is based on three subtasks, the Offensive Language Identification Dataset (OLID), which contains over 14,000 English tweets (Zampieri et al., 2019a). The HASOC track (FIRE 2019) is intended to encourage development in Hate speech identification for Hindi, German, and English language data. For English, HASOC 2019 has 5852 training instances, and 1153 instances for testing and for the Hindi language, the training corpus is 4665, and the testing corpus is 1318 (Mandl et al., 2019a).

4. Results

We begin by examining the accuracy of our tf-idf feature-based machine learning method. We first train the classifiers using tf-idf features. We perform classification on PEI 2019 data, SemEval 2018 task 6 (Zampieri et al., 2019a) and, FIRE 2019 task HASOC (Mandl et al., 2019b) for English datasets and compare our results with other standard benchmarks. We report classification performance of MNB, SGD, LR, and Linear SVM techniques in terms of precision (Pre), recall (Rec), F_1-score, and accuracy where their definitions considered are as given below.

1. Precision: It is the ratio of true-positives (TP) to the sum of true-positives and false-positives (FP).

$$Precision(P) = \frac{TP}{TP + FP} \tag{1}$$

2. Recall: It is the ratio of true-positives (TP) to the sum of true-positives and false-negatives (FN).

$$Recall(R) = \frac{TP}{TP + FN} \tag{2}$$

3. F_1-score: It is the balanced harmonic mean of precision and recall and used to have a composite idea of precision and recall.

$$F_1 = \frac{2 * R * P}{R + P} \tag{3}$$

4. $Macro\_F_1$: It is the average of per-class precision and recall scores over all classes. For each pair of classes, F_1 scores are computed and then arithmetic mean of these per-class F1-scores represent Macro-F_1.

5. $Weighted\_F_1$: It is the weighted version of the average F_1-scores where each class is weighted by the number of samples from that class.

6. Accuracy: It is the ratio of no. of correct predictions to the total number of original entities i.e.

$$Accuracy = \frac{\#\text{ correct predictions}}{\text{Total }\#\text{ test-instances}} \tag{4}$$

[5]https://pypi.org/project/tweet-preprocessor/

[6]https://www.nltk.org/

Table 4: Classifier performance on PEI-2019 for English data

Tasks	**Model**	MNB			SGD			LR			Linear SVM		
	Labels	Pre	Rec	F_1	Pre	Rec	F_1	Pre	Rec	F_1	Pre	Rec	F_1
Sub-task A	HOF	**0.97**	0.21	0.34	0.70	**0.43**	**0.53**	0.91	0.15	0.26	0.68	0.40	0.50
-	NOT	0.81	1.00	0.90	0.85	0.95	0.90	0.80	1.00	0.89	0.84	0.95	0.89
Sub-task B	HATE	**0.50**	0.03	0.05	0.32	0.10	0.15	1.00	0.03	0.05	0.35	0.10	0.16
-	NONE	0.78	1.00	0.88	0.84	0.96	0.89	0.79	1.00	0.88	0.83	0.97	0.89
-	OFFN	0.50	0.02	0.03	**0.85**	**0.61**	**0.71**	1.00	0.09	0.16	0.84	0.46	0.60
Sub-task C	NONE	0.80	0.99	0.88	0.84	0.93	0.88	0.79	0.98	0.88	0.84	0.93	0.88
-	TIN	**0.67**	0.15	0.24	0.55	0.39	**0.45**	0.64	0.13	0.22	0.55	**0.37**	0.44
-	UNT	0.00	0.00	0.00	0.80	0.29	0.42	0.00	0.00	0.00	0.75	0.21	0.33

Table 5: Classifier result of SemEval 2019 task 6 dataset at Precision, Recall, F-score and Accuracy.

Tasks	**Model**	MNB			SGD			LR			Linear SVM		
	Labels	Pre	Rec	F_1	Pre	Rec	F_1	Pre	Rec	F_1	Pre	Rec	F_1
Sub-task A	OFF	0.85	0.15	0.25	**0.92**	0.10	0.18	0.83	0.37	0.51	0.78	**0.46**	**0.58**
-	NOT	0.70	0.99	0.82	0.69	1.00	0.82	0.76	0.96	0.85	0.78	0.94	0.85
Sub-task B	GRP	0.00	0.00	0.00	0.00	0.00	0.00	**0.50**	0.03	0.06	0.48	0.05	0.10
-	IND	0.83	0.01	0.02	1.00	0.00	0.01	0.65	0.14	0.23	0.65	0.23	0.34
-	NULL	0.69	1.00	0.82	0.69	1.00	0.82	0.72	0.99	0.83	0.73	0.98	0.84
-	OTH	0.00	0.00	0.00	0.00	0.00	0.00	0.00	0.00	0.00	0.00	0.00	0.00
Sub-task C	NULL	0.69	0.99	0.81	0.68	1.00	0.81	0.73	0.97	0.83	0.76	0.94	0.84
-	TIN	**0.77**	0.10	0.17	0.73	0.04	0.08	0.72	0.28	0.40	0.67	**0.39**	0.49
-	UNT	0.00	0.00	0.00	0.00	0.00	0.00	0.00	0.00	0.00	0.00	0.00	0.00

Table 6: Classifier result of FIRE 2019 task HASOC dataset at Precision, Recall, F-score and Accuracy.

Tasks	**Model**	MNB			SGD			LR			Linear SVM		
	Labels	Pre	Rec	F_1	Pre	Rec	F_1	Precision	Recall	F_1	Pre	Rec	F_1
Sub-task A	HOF	0.70	0.18	0.29	0.78	0.07	0.12	0.67	0.28	0.40	0.64	0.36	0.46
-	NOT	0.64	0.95	0.76	0.62	0.99	0.76	0.66	0.91	0.77	0.68	0.87	0.76
Sub-task B	HATE	0.00	0.00	0.00	0.00	0.00	0.00	0.29	0.03	0.05	0.29	0.06	0.10
-	NONE	0.62	1.00	0.77	0.63	1.00	0.77	0.64	0.98	0.78	0.65	0.95	0.77
-	OFFN	0.00	0.00	0.00	0.00	0.00	0.00	0.60	0.03	0.06	0.57	0.08	0.14
-	PRFN	0.86	0.04	0.07	0.78	0.12	0.20	0.78	0.12	0.20	0.79	0.18	0.29
Sub-task C	NONE	0.65	0.96	0.77	0.64	1.00	0.78	0.67	0.92	0.78	0.68	0.87	0.76
-	TIN	0.65	0.14	0.23	0.86	0.06	0.12	0.64	0.26	0.37	0.57	0.34	0.43
-	UNT	0.00	0.00	0.00	0.00	0.00	0.00	0.00	0.00	0.00	0.00	0.00	0.00

Table 7: Classifier result on testing dataset of PEI data

Task/Model	Sub-task A			Sub-task B			Sub-task C		
Model	Mac_f1	W_f1	Accuracy	Mac_f1	W_f1	Accuracy	Mac_f1	W_f1	Accuracy
Multinomial_NB	0.62	0.77	0.82	0.32	0.69	0.78	0.37	0.73	0.79
SGD	0.71	0.81	0.83	0.59	0.78	0.82	0.59	0.79	0.80
LR	0.58	0.75	0.81	0.36	0.70	0.79	0.37	0.73	0.79
Linear SVM	0.70	0.81	0.82	0.55	0.77	0.81	0.55	0.78	0.80

Table 8: Classifier result on testing dataset of SemEval 2019 Task 6 dataset

Task/Model	Subtask A			Subtask B			Subtask C		
Model	Mac_f1	W_f1	Accuracy	Mac_f1	W_f1	Accuracy	Mac_f1	W_f1	Accuracy
Multinomial_NB	0.54	0.63	0.71	0.33	0.59	0.69	0.21	0.57	0.69
SGD	0.50	0.61	0.70	0.30	0.56	0.68	0.21	0.57	0.69
LR	0.68	0.74	0.77	0.41	0.67	0.73	0.28	0.62	0.71
Linear SVM	0.71	0.76	0.78	0.44	0.70	0.74	0.32	0.65	0.72

Table 4 shows the result of PEI-2019 dataset for English. The machine learning models performed way better for PEI data than for the SemEval data-set. The reason is domain-specificity. While PEI dataset

Table 9: Classifier result on testing dataset of FIRE 2019 HASOC task dataset

Task/Model	Sub-task A			Sub-task B			Sub-task C		
Model	Mac_f1	W_f1	Accuracy	Mac_f1	W_f1	Accuracy	Mac_f1	W_f1	Accuracy
Multinomial_NB	0.53	0.58	0.65	0.21	0.49	0.62	0.33	0.56	0.65
SGD	0.44	0.51	0.62	0.24	0.51	0.63	0.30	0.52	0.64
LR	0.58	0.62	0.66	0.29	0.53	0.64	0.38	0.61	0.67
Linear SVM	0.61	0.64	0.67	0.35	0.56	0.64	0.40	0.62	0.66

Table 10: Classifier result of PEI-2019 dataset at Precision, Recall, F-score and Accuracy for Hindi data

Tasks	**Model**	MNB			SGD			LR			Linear SVM		
	Labels	Pre	Rec	F_1	Pre	Rec	F_1	Precision	Recall	F_1	Pre	Rec	F_1
Sub-task A	HOF	**0.85**	0.38	0.52	0.73	**0.64**	**0.68**	0.78	0.39	0.52	0.75	0.61	0.67
-	NOT	0.72	0.96	0.83	0.80	0.87	0.83	0.72	0.94	0.82	0.79	0.88	0.83
Sub-task B	HATE	0.33	0.02	0.04	0.59	0.34	0.43	0.57	0.17	0.26	0.63	0.36	0.46
-	NONE	0.64	0.99	0.78	0.76	0.93	0.83	0.68	0.98	0.80	0.73	0.96	0.83
-	OFFN	0.00	0.00	0.00	0.41	0.28	0.33	0.00	0.00	0.00	0.71	0.20	0.31
Sub-task C	NONE	0.73	0.98	0.84	0.81	0.89	0.84	0.75	0.98	0.85	0.82	0.91	0.86
-	TIN	0.79	0.30	0.44	0.67	0.59	0.63	0.81	0.35	0.49	0.72	0.60	0.66
-	UNT	0.00	0.00	0.00	0.00	0.00	0.00	0.00	0.00	0.00	0.00	0.00	0.00

Table 11: Classifier result on testing dataset of PEI Hindi data

Task/Model	Sub-task A			Sub-task B			Sub-task C		
Model	Mac_f1	W_f1	Accuracy	Mac_f1	W_f1	Accuracy	Mac_f1	W_f1	Accuracy
Multinomial_NB	0.67	0.71	0.74	0.20	0.50	0.64	0.42	0.69	0.74
SGD	**0.76**	**0.78**	**0.78**	**0.40**	0.67	0.70	0.49	0.76	0.77
LR	0.67	0.71	0.735	0.27	0.57	0.67	0.44	0.71	0.76
Linear_SV	0.75	0.77	**0.78**	**0.40**	**0.68**	**0.72**	**0.51**	**0.77**	**0.79**

is specific to election domain, SemEval contains posts from diverse domains. This affects the learning accuracy of the models, and hence PEI-2019 dataset performs better.

Table 5 and 8 show results of SemEval 2019 Task 6 dataset for English. The highest accuracy scores are 0.78, 0.74 and 0.72 for Subtask A, Subtask B and subtask C respectively.

We participated in FIRE 2019 (Saroj et al., 2019), and obtained the accuracy of XGBoost (81%) better than that of SVM (73%) for Subtask A (similar to Task A). The accuracy for Sub-task B and Sub-task C are the same for the XGBoost (80%). Table 6 and 9 show the FIRE HASOC English dataset results with accuracy 0.67, 0.64, 67 Subtask A, Subtask B and Subtask C respectively, where Mac_f1 is macro_f1 and W_f1 is weighted_f1.
The results above show that classification performance of PEI 2019 dataset is much better than the other dataset that are compared with for any of the techniques. In linear regression (LR), the macro-averaged F_1-score is 0.68 for SemEval 2019 dataset and 0.58 for the PEI 2019 dataset and FIRE 2019 dataset listed in Table 4, 5, and 6 respectively. The results of these experiments listed in Table 7, 8, and 9. Among the techniques, accuracy of the SGD classifier is the best among the three tasks (Task A, B, and C).

Table 10 and 11 show classification results for Hindi. The highest accuracy for Task A is 0.78 on SGD by linear SVM. For Tasks B and C, the highest accuracy are 0.72 and 0.79 respectively, again, by linear SVM.

5. Discussion

We found the highest accuracy in SGD classifier for all three subtasks in English data. For Hindi Linear SVM gives the best accuracy for all classes. LR gives better score in SemEval 2019 dataset compared to PEI 2019 and HASOC dataset. Multinomial NB, SGD, and Linear SVM give better F_1 score and accuracy in PEI 2019 dataset in all three subtasks than other datasets.

6. Conclusion

In this paper, we introduced a dataset for hate speech and offensive content detection in Indian language and Indian context. We tested a number of text classification techniques to recognize hate speech and offensive posts to validate our dataset: Multinomial Naive-Bayes, Stochastic Gradient Descent, Logistic Regression, and Linear Support Vector. The best results are achieved by Stochastic Gradient Descent (SGD), achieving 83% accuracy in three subtasks. We believe that tackling hate and offensive content in social media is a serious challenge and our PEI dataset will be useful, specifically in Indian context as it the first such dataset in any Indian language. In the future, we'd like to apply domain adaptation and joint training from the parliamentary election 2019 of India.

7. References

Britannica, E. (2015). Britannica academic. *Encyclopædia Britannica Inc.*

Dr. Jakob Jünger, T. K. (2019). Facepager. *An application for generic data retrieval through APIs.*

Malmasi, S. and Zampieri, M. (2017). Detecting hate speech in social media. *arXiv preprint arXiv:1712.06427.*

Mandl, T., Modha, S., Majumder, P., Patel, D., Dave, M., Mandlia, C., and Patel, A. (2019a). Overview of the hasoc track at fire 2019: Hate speech and offensive content identification in indo-european languages. In *Proceedings of the 11th Forum for Information Retrieval Evaluation*, pages 14–17.

Mandl, T., Modha, S., Patel, D., Dave, M., Mandlia, C., and Patel, A. (2019b). Overview of the HASOC track at FIRE 2019: Hate Speech and Offensive Content Identification in Indo-European Languages). In *Proceedings of the 11th annual meeting of the Forum for Information Retrieval Evaluation.*

Ramakrishnan, M., Zadrozny, W., and Tabari, N. (2019). UVA wahoos at SemEval-2019 task 6: Hate speech identification using ensemble machine learning. In *Proceedings of the 13th International Workshop on Semantic Evaluation*, pages 806–811, Minneapolis, Minnesota, USA, June. Association for Computational Linguistics.

Saroj, A., Mundotiya, R. K., and Pal, S. (2019). Irlab@ iitbhu at hasoc 2019: Traditional machine learning for hate speech and offensive content identification.

Zampieri, M., Malmasi, S., Nakov, P., Rosenthal, S., Farra, N., and Kumar, R. (2019a). Semeval-2019 task 6: Identifying and categorizing offensive language in social media (offenseval). *arXiv preprint arXiv:1903.08983.*

Zampieri, M., Malmasi, S., Nakov, P., Rosenthal, S., Farra, N., and Kumar, R. (2019b). Semeval-2019 task 6: Identifying and categorizing offensive language in social media (offenseval). In *Proceedings of the 13th International Workshop on Semantic Evaluation*, pages 75–86.

Resources and Techniques for User and Author Profiling in Abusive Language (ResT-UP 2020), pages 9–13
Language Resources and Evaluation Conference (LREC 2020), Marseille, 11–16 May 2020

Profiling Italian Misogynist: An Empirical Study

Elisabetta Fersini, Debora Nozza, Giulia Boifava
University of Milano-Bicocca, Bocconi University, University of Milano-Bicocca
elisabetta.fersini@unimib.it, debora.nozza@unibocconi.it, g.boifava1@campus.unimib.it

Abstract

Hate speech may take different forms in online social environments. In this paper, we address the problem of automatic detection of misogynous language on Italian tweets by focusing both on raw text and stylometric profiles. The proposed exploratory investigation about the adoption of stylometry for enhancing the recognition capabilities of machine learning models has demonstrated that profiling users can lead to good discrimination of misogynous and not misogynous contents.

Keywords: Automatic Misogyny Identification, Stylometry

1. Introduction

The problem of identifying misogynist language in online social contexts has recently attracted significant attention. Social networks need to update their policy to address this issue and due to the high volume of texts shared daily, the automatic detection of misogynist and sexist text content is required. However, the problem of automatic misogyny identification from a linguistic point of view is still in its early stage. In particular, trivial statistics about the usage of misogynous language in Twitter have been provided in (Hewitt et al., 2016), while in (Anzovino et al., 2018) a first tentative of defining linguistic features and machine learning models for automatically recognizing this phenomenon has been presented. Given this relevant social problem, several shared tasks have been recently proposed for different languages (i.e. Italian, Spanish and English) to discriminate misogynous and not misogynous contents, demonstrating the interest of the Natural Language Processing community on investigating the linguistic and communication behaviour of this phenomenon. The Automatic Misogyny Identification (AMI) challenge (Fersini et al., 2018a; Fersini et al., 2018b) has been proposed at Ibereval 2018[1] for Spanish and English, and in Evalita 2018 (Caselli et al., 2018) for Italian and English. The main goal of AMI is to distinguish misogynous contents from non-misogynous ones, to categorize misogynistic behaviors and finally to classify the target of a tweet. Afterwards, (Basile et al., 2019) proposed HatEval, the shared task at SemEval 2019 on multilingual detection of hate speech against immigrants and women in Twitter for Spanish and English. The aim of HatEval is to detect the presence of hate speech against immigrants and women, and to identify further features in hateful contents such as the aggressive attitude and the target harassed, to distinguish if the incitement is against an individual rather than a group. This challenges offered the unique opportunity to firstly address the problem of hate speech against women in online social networks.

2. State of the art

During the above mentioned challenges, several systems have been presented to obtain the best performing solution in terms of recognition performance. Most of the participants to the AMI challenge considered a single type of text representation, i.e. traditional TF-IDF representation, while (Bakarov, 2018) and (Buscaldi, 2018) considered only weighted n-grams at character level for better dealing with misspellings and capturing few stylistic aspects. Additionally to the traditional textual feature representation techniques, i.e. bag of words/characters, n-grams of words/characters eventually weighted with TF-IDF, several approaches used specific lexical features for improving the input space and consequently the classification performances. In (Basile and Rubagotti, 2018) the authors experimented feature abstraction following the bleaching approach proposed by Goot et al. (Goot et al., 2018) for modelling gender through the language. Finally, specific lexicons for dealing with hate speech language have been included as features in several approaches (Frenda et al., 2018), (Ahluwalia et al., 2018) and (Pamungkas et al., 2018). Few participants to the AMI challenge, (Fortuna et al., 2018) and (Saha et al., 2018) considered the popular Embeddings techniques both at word and sentence level. More recently, (Nozza et al., 2019) investigated the use of a novel Deep Learning Representation model, the *Universal Sentence Encoder* introduced in (Cer et al., 2018) built using a transformer architecture (Vaswani et al., 2017) for tweet representation. The use of this more sophisticated model for textual representation coupled with a simple single-layer neural network architecture allowed the authors to outperform the first-ranked approach (Saha et al., 2018) at Evalita 2018. Thus, in the HatEval challenge, more than half of the participants exploited Word Embeddings or Deep Learning models (Sabour et al., 2017; Cer et al., 2018) for textual representation.

Concerning the machine learning models, the majority of the available investigations in the state of the art are usually based on traditional Support Vector Machines and Deep Learning methods, mainly Recurrent Neural Networks.

Several works have been done for adopting or even enlarging some lexical resources for misogyny detection purposes. The lexicons for addressing misogyny detection for the Italian language have been mostly obtained from lists available online, i.e. "Le parole per ferire" given by Tullio De Mauro[2], and the HurtLex multilingual lexicon (Bassignana et al., 2018).

[1] https://sites.google.com/view/ibereval-2018

[2] https://www.internazionale.it/opinione/tullio-de-mauro/2016/09/27/razzismo-parole-ferire

Although the above mentioned approaches represent a fundamental step towards the definition of mechanisms able to distinguish between misogynous and not misogynous contents, it is still pending the verification of the hypothesis that the writing style of authors could be a strong indication of misogynous profiles that therefore are likely inclined to produce misogynous contents.
To this purpose, in this paper, we propose to investigate the ability of some stylometric features to characterize misogynous and not misogynous profiles.

3. The Proposed Approach

The traditional feature vector representing a message m (used to train a given classifier) usually includes only terms that belong to a common vocabulary V of terms derived from a message collection:

$$\vec{m} = (w_1, w_2, ..., w_{|V|}, l) \quad (1)$$

where w_t denotes the weight of term t belonging to m with label l. However, some stylometric signals can be used to enhance the traditional feature vector and therefore learning models to distinguish between misogynous and not misogynous contents. The expanded feature vector of a message is defined as:

$$\vec{m}_s = (w_1, w_2, ..., w_{|V|}, s_1, s_2, \ldots, s_n, l) \quad (2)$$

where $s_1, s_2, \ldots, s_n$ represent the n additional stylometric features. The stylometric features investigate in this paper can be broadly distinguished as follow:

- *Pragmatic particles*: to better capture non-literal signals that could convey misogynous expressions, several valuable pragmatic forms could be taken into account. Pragmatic particles, such as emoticons, mentions and hashtags expressions, represent those linguistic elements typically used on social ratio to elicit, remark and make direct a given message.
- *Punctuation*: as stated in (Watanabe et al., 2018), how an internet user uses exclamation, interjections, and other punctuation marks is not necessarily an explicit cue indicating misogyny, they can be used to implicitly elicit a misogynous message (e.g. "Women rights? come on...go back to the kitchen!!!").
- *Part-Of-Speech (POS) lexical components*: the way of using some specific part of speech could be a relevant indicator of misogyny. For this reason, a POS tagger could be applied in order to assign lexical functions and derive some stylometric features related to them.

The above mentioned stylometric categories have led us to investigate the following features as candidates to capture misogynous profile and therefore to be included as additional features s_i reported in Eq. (2):

- average number of sentences
- average number of words
- frequency of the number of unique words
- frequency of complex words (more than 5 characters)
- average of the number of characters in a word
- frequency of the number of verbs
- frequency of the number of auxiliary verbs
- frequency of the number of adjectives
- frequency of the number of superlative adjectives
- frequency of the number of superlative relative adjectives
- frequency the number of comparative adjectives
- frequency of the number of nouns
- frequency of the number of conjunctions
- frequency of the number of adverbs
- frequency of articles
- frequency of indefinite articles
- frequency of definite articles
- frequency of indefinite articles prepositions
- frequency of pronouns
- frequency of numbers
- frequency of special characters
- frequency of emoji
- frequency of unigrams
- frequency of bigrams
- frequency of trigrams
- frequency of offensive words
- frequency of punctuation
- frequency of commas
- frequency of colon
- frequency of semi-comma
- frequency of exclamation mark
- frequency of question mark
- frequency of quotes
- frequency of upper-case words
- frequency of words starting with upper case
- frequency of stretched words
- frequency of the first singular person pronouns
- frequency of the first plural person pronouns
- frequency of the second singular person pronouns

- frequency of the second plural person pronouns
- frequency of the third singular person pronouns related to male
- frequency of the third singular person pronouns related to female
- frequency of the third plural person pronouns related to male
- frequency of the third plural person pronouns related to female
- frequency of the # symbol
- frequency of the @ symbol
- frequency of proper nouns

To validate the hypothesis that a stylistic profile can help to detect misogynous contents from the not misogynous ones, we trained several machine learning models both on the traditional feature vector (Eq. 1) and on the expanded feature vector (Eq. 2).

4. Experimental Investigation

4.1. Dataset

In order to validate our hypothesis that a stylistic profile of Italian misogynist can improve the generalization capabilities of machine learning models trained for misogyny detection purposes, we adopted the Italian benchmark dataset provided for the AMI@Evalita Challenge. The dataset has been collected by following the subsequent policies:

- Streaming download using a set of representative keywords, e.g. *pu****a, tr**a, f**a di legno*
- Monitoring of potential victims' accounts, e.g. *gamergate victims and public feminist women*
- Downloading the history of identified misogynist, i.e. *explicitly declared hate against women on their Twitter profiles*

The annotated Italian corpus is finally composed of 5000 tweets, almost balanced between misogynous and not misogynous labels.

4.2. Models and Performance Measures

Concerning the machine learning models trained to distinguish between misogynous and not misogynous tweets, Naïve Bayes (NB), Support Vector Machines (SVM) and Multi-Layer Perceptron (MLP) have been adopted[3].
Regarding the *traditional feature vector*, the text of each tweet has been stemmed and its TF-IDF representation has been obtained by exploiting the *sklearn* library (Pedregosa et al., 2011). For the stylometric features, we employed the Italian models of the *spaCy* library to obtain the part-of-speech tags to collect nouns, adjectives, adverbs. We also created a manual list of prepositions and articles. The list of offensive words has been extracted from an online resource [4].
Concerning the experimental evaluation, a 10-folds cross validation has been performed. To compare the two feature spaces, traditional textual feature vector and the ones with additional stylometric features, *Precision*, *Recall* and *F1-measure* have been estimated focusing on both labels (i.e. 0=notMisogynous, 1=misogynous).

4.3. Experimental Results

We report in Table 1 the experimental results obtained by training all the considered machine learning models on the two feature space, i.e. the first based on Tf-IDF only and the second one based on TF-IDF and stylometric features.
We can easily note that the stylometric features provide a strong contribution for discriminating between misogynous and not misogynous messages. It is interesting to note that the stylometric features are not only able to improve the performance with respect to the traditional features, but they lead to have good performance for both classes guarantying a good compromise of Precision and Recall for misogynous and not misogynous instances. In this way, we are able to provide a feature representation and a machine learning approach that is able to recognize "the easy class" related to not misogynous contents and "the difficult class" related to the misogynous text. In order to better understand the role of stylometric cues, we performed an error analysis on those messages that were wrongly classified by the best performing model, i.e. Support Vector Machines. First of all, the proposed analysis involving stylometry has led to 20% of classification error, where 43.85% of misclassified instances are not misogynous tweets that are classified as misogynous and 56.15% of misclassified instances are misogynous tweets that are classified as not misogynous.
For those instances for which the actual label was not misogynous but the classifier predicted them as misogynous, we can highlight the main types of errors:

- *Unsolved Mentions*: the model, do not solving the user mentions, is biased by adjectives. In particular, when referring to a target by using a mention (denote by the @ symbol), the stylometric features are not able to capture the gender-related to a given noun and therefore is biased by the bad words typically related to women. An example of this type of errors are represented by the following sentence:

  *@laltrodiego Mer*a schifosa lurida*

  that can be translated as:

  *@laltrodiego Bad Sh*tty Sh*t*

  The target of the tweet is an account of a male user, but the model do not have the chance to solve the uncertainty related to the mention.

- *Wrong Target*: in this case, the model is again biased by adjectives typically denoting bad words because it is not able to recognize female proper nouns. In particular, when mentioning a given entity (i.e. football

[3]The experiments have been conducted using default parameters of models implemented in sklearn: https://scikit-learn.org

[4]https://bit.ly/2HK3fYE

		Precision		Recall		F1-Measure	
		0	1	0	1	0	1
TD-IDF	NB	0.816	0.459	0.381	0.858	0.519	0.598
	MLP	0.840	0.745	0.844	0.735	0.841	0.738
	SVM	0.839	0.713	0.811	0.746	0.823	0.727
TF-IDF + stylometry	NB	0.816	0.524	0.559	0.793	0.662	0.631
	MLP	0.851	0.810	0.888	0.743	0.868	0.773
	SVM	0.910	0.747	0.793	0.848	0.835	0.777

Table 1: Experimental results

teams, male, locations) the stylometric features are not able to capture the gender and therefore the model is again biased by the bad words typically related to women. An example of this type of errors are represented by the following sentence:

> *Sintesi: Barcellona cul*na, De Rossi come CR7. Entrambi applauditi dai tifosi avversari. #BarcaRoma #BarcellonaRoma*

that can be translated as:

> *Summary: Barcelona big a*s, De Rossi as CR7. Both applauded by the opposing fans. #BarcaRoma #BarcelonaRoma*

The target of the tweet relates to a football team and not on a female user, but the model does not have the chance to solve the uncertainty related to the target.

- *Absence of an Explicit Target*: in this case, the model misclassify those tweets where the target is not explicitly stated. Typical examples are comments related to events, where offensive words related to female are used to complain:

  > *PORCA PUT**NA LADRA SCHIFOSA IERI HARRY STYLES ERA NELLA MIA CITTA E IO NON SAPEVO NULLA.HARRY STYLES ERA A MODENA E IO LO AVREI POTUTO INCONTRARE, ODIO TUTTI CHE VITA DI MER*A*

  that can be translated as:

  > *SHITTY BIT*H YESTERDAY HARRY STYLES WAS IN MY CITY AND I DID NOT KNOW ANYTHING.HARRY STYLES WAS IN MODENA AND I WOULD HAVE BEEN ABLE TO MEET HIM, I HATE ALL WHAT A SHIT*Y LIFE*

  In this case, the implicit target is an event and the model, observing offensive words such as *putt*na/bit*h* wrongly predict the message as misogynous.

An analogous behaviour has been observed when the actual labels of tweets are misogynous but the classifier predicted them as not misogynous. In particular, the errors are mainly related to one main lack of information:

- *Absence of Syntactic Features*: the model, which does not consider the syntactical structure of the sentence, is not able to determine the target of an offensive adjective. An example of these types of errors are represented by the following sentence:

  > *Se scrivi che Weinstein o Trump sono dei porci e dei maniaci tutti applaudono, ma se dici che Selvaggia Lucarelli è un putt*none sei sessista...*

  that can be translated as:

  > *If you write that Weinstein or Trump are pigs and maniacs everyone applauds, but if you say that Selvaggia Lucarelli is a bit*h you're sexist ...*

  The target of the offensive language is clearly a woman, but the model since it does not consider the structure of the sentence it is biased by those adjectives related to men.

The error analysis has highlighted on one side the necessity of properly dealing with the target of the message, and on the other hand, it has pointed out the needs to more additional stylometric features to obtain a better understanding on the structuring of sentences of both misogynous and not misogynous contents.

4.4. Conclusions and Future Work

In this paper, a preliminary empirical investigation about the profiling of Italian misogynous contents has been performed. A set of stylometric features have been studied for validating the hypothesis that cues about the writing style of authors can contribute to better distinguish misogynous contents from the not misogynous ones. The experimental evaluation has corroborated the hypothesis that the use of stylometric features improves the recognition capabilities of several machine learning models for misogyny detection purposes. Concerning future work, several additional syntactic features will be considered for a better understanding of the structure of the sentences. Additionally, the capabilities of the investigated features will be evaluated focusing on additional languages, i.e. Spanish and English, also investigating which set of features contributes most on the results of the classifiers. As final future work, a different paradigm for profiling misogynist will be investigated. In particular, a benchmark profile of misogynistic and not misogynistic language will be created to then enable a *learning-by-difference* approach.

5. Bibliographical References

Ahluwalia, R., Soni, H., Callow, E., Nascimento, A., and Cock, M. D. (2018). Detecting Hate Speech Against Women in English Tweets. In *Proceedings of Sixth Evaluation Campaign of Natural Language Processing and Speech Tools for Italian. Final Workshop (EVALITA 2018)*, Turin, Italy. CEUR.org.

Anzovino, M., Fersini, E., and Rosso, P. (2018). Automatic Identification and Classification of Misogynistic Language on Twitter. In *International Conference on Applications of Natural Language to Information Systems*, pages 57–64. Springer.

Bakarov, A. (2018). Vector Space Models for Automatic Misogyny Identification. In *Proceedings of Sixth Evaluation Campaign of Natural Language Processing and Speech Tools for Italian. Final Workshop (EVALITA 2018)*, Turin, Italy. CEUR.org.

Basile, A. and Rubagotti, C. (2018). Automatic Identification of Misogyny in English and Italian Tweets at EVALITA 2018 with a Multilingual Hate Lexicon. In *Proceedings of Sixth Evaluation Campaign of Natural Language Processing and Speech Tools for Italian. Final Workshop (EVALITA 2018)*, Turin, Italy. CEUR.org.

Basile, V., Bosco, C., Fersini, E., Nozza, D., Patti, V., Rangel, F., Rosso, P., and Sanguinetti, M. (2019). Semeval-2019 task 5: Multilingual detection of hate speech against immigrants and women in twitter. In *Proceedings of the 13th International Workshop on Semantic Evaluation (SemEval-2019)*. Association for Computational Linguistics.

Bassignana, E., Basile, V., and Patti, V. (2018). Hurtlex: A multilingual lexicon of words to hurt. In *5th Italian Conference on Computational Linguistics, CLiC-it 2018*, volume 2253, pages 1–6. CEUR-WS.

Buscaldi, D. (2018). Tweetaneuse AMI EVALITA2018: Character-based Models for the Automatic Misogyny Identification Task. In *Proceedings of Sixth Evaluation Campaign of Natural Language Processing and Speech Tools for Italian. Final Workshop (EVALITA 2018)*, Turin, Italy. CEUR.org.

Caselli, T., Novielli, N., Patti, V., and Rosso, P. (2018). EVALITA 2018: Overview of the 6th Evaluation Campaign of Natural Language Processing and Speech Tools for Italian. In Tommaso Caselli, et al., editors, *Proceedings of Sixth Evaluation Campaign of Natural Language Processing and Speech Tools for Italian. Final Workshop (EVALITA 2018)*, Turin, Italy. CEUR.org.

Cer, D., Yang, Y., Kong, S.-y., Hua, N., Limtiaco, N., St. John, R., Constant, N., Guajardo-Cespedes, M., Yuan, S., Tar, C., Strope, B., and Kurzweil, R. (2018). Universal sentence encoder for English. In *Proceedings of the 2018 Conference on Empirical Methods in Natural Language Processing: System Demonstrations (EMNLP 2018)*, pages 169–174. Association for Computational Linguistics, November.

Fersini, E., Nozza, D., and Rosso, P. (2018a). Overview of the Evalita 2018 Task on Automatic Misogyny Identification (AMI). In Tommaso Caselli, et al., editors, *Proceedings of the 6th evaluation campaign of Natural Language Processing and Speech tools for Italian (EVALITA'18)*, Turin, Italy. CEUR.org.

Fersini, E., Rosso, P., and Anzovino, M. (2018b). Overview of the Task on Automatic Misogyny Identification at IberEval 2018. In *Proceedings of the Third Workshop on Evaluation of Human Language Technologies for Iberian Languages (IberEval 2018)*. CEUR-WS.org.

Fortuna, P., Bonavita, I., and Nunes, S. (2018). INESC TEC, Eurecat and Porto University.

Frenda, S., Ghanem, B., Guzmán-Falcón, E., Montes-y-Gómez, M., and Villaseñor-Pineda, L. (2018). Automatic Lexicons Expansion for Multilingual Misogyny Detection. In *Proceedings of Sixth Evaluation Campaign of Natural Language Processing and Speech Tools for Italian. Final Workshop (EVALITA 2018)*, Turin, Italy. CEUR.org.

Goot, R., Ljubešić, N., Matroos, I., Nissim, M., and Plank, B. (2018). Bleaching Text: Abstract Features for Cross-lingual Gender Prediction. In *Proceedings of the 56th Annual Meeting of the Association for Computational Linguistics (Volume 2: Short Papers)*, volume 2, pages 383–389.

Hewitt, S., Tiropanis, T., and Bokhove, C. (2016). The Problem of identifying Misogynist Language on Twitter (and other online social spaces). In *Proceedings of the 8th ACM Conference on Web Science*, pages 333–335. ACM.

Nozza, D., Volpetti, C., and Fersini, E. (2019). Unintended bias in misogyny detection. In *IEEE/WIC/ACM International Conference on Web Intelligence*, pages 149–155.

Pamungkas, E. W., Cignarella, A. T., Basile, V., and Patti, V. (2018). Automatic Identification of Misogyny in English and Italian Tweets at EVALITA 2018 with a Multilingual Hate Lexicon. In *Proceedings of Sixth Evaluation Campaign of Natural Language Processing and Speech Tools for Italian. Final Workshop (EVALITA 2018)*, Turin, Italy. CEUR.org.

Pedregosa, F., Varoquaux, G., Gramfort, A., Michel, V., Thirion, B., Grisel, O., Blondel, M., Prettenhofer, P., Weiss, R., Dubourg, V., Vanderplas, J., Passos, A., Cournapeau, D., Brucher, M., Perrot, M., and Duchesnay, E. (2011). Scikit-learn: Machine learning in Python. *Journal of Machine Learning Research*, 12:2825–2830.

Sabour, S., Frosst, N., and Hinton, G. E. (2017). Dynamic routing between capsules. In *Advances in neural information processing systems*, pages 3856–3866.

Saha, P., Mathew, B., Goyal, P., and Mukherjee, A. (2018). Indian Institute of Engineering Science and Technology (Shibpur), Indian Institute of Technology (Kharagpur).

Vaswani, A., Shazeer, N., Parmar, N., Uszkoreit, J., Jones, L., Gomez, A. N., Kaiser, L., and Polosukhin, I. (2017). Attention is All you Need. In *Advances in Neural Information Processing Systems 30: Annual Conference on Neural Information Processing Systems (NIPS 2017)*, pages 6000–6010.

Watanabe, H., Bouazizi, M., and Ohtsuki, T. (2018). Hate speech on twitter: A pragmatic approach to collect hateful and offensive expressions and perform hate speech detection. *IEEE Access*, 6:13825–13835.

Resources and Techniques for User and Author Profiling in Abusive Language (ResT-UP 2020), pages 14–19
Language Resources and Evaluation Conference (LREC 2020), Marseille, 11–16 May 2020

Lower Bias, Higher Density Abusive Language Datasets: A Recipe

Juliet van Rosendaal, Tommaso Caselli, Malvina Nissim
University of Groningen
Oude Kijk in't Jaatstraat, 26 9712 EK Groningen
julietlucienne@msn.com, {t.caselli,m.nissim}@rug.nl

Abstract

Datasets to train models for abusive language detection are both necessary and scarce. One reason for their limited availability is the cost of their creation. Manual annotation is expensive, and on top of it, the phenomenon itself is sparse, causing human annotators having to go through a large number of irrelevant examples in order to obtain some significant data. Strategies used until now to increase density of abusive language and obtain more meaningful data, include data filtering on the basis of pre-selected keywords and hate-rich sources of data. We suggest a recipe that at the same time can provide meaningful data with possibly higher density of abusive language and also reduce top-down biases imposed by corpus creators in the selection of the data to annotate. More specifically, we exploit the controversy channel on Reddit to obtain keywords that are used to filter a Twitter dataset. While the method needs further validation and refinement, our preliminary experiments show a higher density of abusive tweets in the filtered *vs.* unfiltered datasets, and a more meaningful topic distribution after filtering.

1. Problem Statement

The automatic detection of abusive and offensive messages in on-line communities has become a pressing issue. The promise of Social Media to create a more open and connected world is challenged by the growth of abusive behaviors, among which cyberbullying, trolling, and hate speech are some of the most known. It has also been shown that awareness of being a victim of some kind of abusive behavior is less widespread than what one actually reports as having experienced (Jurgens et al., 2019).

The body of work conducted in the areas of abusive language, hate speech, and offensive language has rapidly grown in the last years, leaving the field with a variety of definitions and a lack of reflection on the intersection among such different phenomena (Waseem et al., 2017; Vidgen et al., 2019). As a direct consequence, there has been a flood of annotated datasets in different languages, [1] all somehow addressing the same phenomena (e.g. offensive language, or hate speech) but applying slightly different definitions, different annotation approaches (e.g. experts *vs.* crowdsourcing), and different reference domains (e.g., Twitter, Facebook, Reddit). Hate speech, in particular, has been the target of the latest major evaluation campaigns such as SemEval 2019 (Zampieri et al., 2019b; Basile et al., 2019), EVALITA 2018 (Bosco et al., 2018), and IberEVAL 2018 (Fersini et al., 2018) in an attempt to promote both the development of working systems and a better understanding of the phenomenon.

Vidgen et al. (2019) and Jurgens et al. (2019) identify a set of pending issues that require attention and care by people in NLP working on this topic. One of them concerns a revision of what actually constitutes abuse. The perspective that has been adopted so far in the definition of abusive language, and most importantly of hate speech, has been limited to specific and narrow types of abusive/hateful behaviors to recognize. For instance, definitions of hate speech have been carefully carved, focusing on the intentions of the message producer and by listing cases of applications (e.g., attack against an individual or a group on the basis of race, religion, ethnic origin, sexual orientation, disability, or gender). As a consequence, more subtle but still debasing and harmful cases are excluded, and (potential) negative effects of the messages on the targets are neither considered nor accounted for.

A further problematic aspect in previous work concerns the quality of the datasets. Besides issues on the annotation efforts (i.e., amount of data and selected annotation approach), one outstanding problem is the collection of data. While some language phenomena are widespread in any (social media) text one may collect (e.g. presence of named entities), hate speech is not. Random sampling from targeted platforms is thus a non-viable solution as it will entail going through a large amount of non-hateful messages before finding, very sparse, hateful cases. To circumvent this obstacle, three main strategies have been adopted so far:

- use of communities (Tulkens et al., 2016; Merenda et al., 2018): potentially hateful or abusive messages are extracted by collecting data from on-line communities that are known either to promote or tolerate such types of messages;
- use of keywords (Waseem and Hovy, 2016; Basile et al., 2019; Zampieri et al., 2019a): specific keywords which are not hateful or abusive *per se* but that may be the target of hateful or abusive messages, like for instance the word "migrants", are selected to collect random messages from Social Media outlets;
- use of users (Wiegand et al., 2018; Ribeiro et al., 2018): seed users that have been identified via some heuristics to regularly post abusive or hateful materials are selected and their messages collected. In a variation of this approach, additional potential "hateful" users are identified by applying network analysis to the seed users.

[1] For a more detailed overview of available datasets in different languages please consult `https://github.com/leondz/hatespeechdata`.

Common advantages of these approaches mainly lie in the reduction of annotation time and a higher density of positive instances, i.e. hateful messages in our case. However, a common and non-negligible downside is the developer's bias that unavoidably seeps in the datasets, although with varying levels of impact. For instance, it has been shown that Waseem and Hovy (2016) is a particularly skewed datasets with respect to topics and authors (Wiegand et al., 2019). For instance, words such as "commentator", "comedian", or "football" have strong correlations with hateful messages, or that hateful messages are mainly distributed across 3 different authors.

In this contribution, we present a simple data-driven method towards the creation of a corpus for hate speech annotation. We apply it to Dutch, a less resourced language for this phenomenon, but the method can be conceived as a blueprint to be applied to any other language for which social media data are available.

Our approach exploits cross-information from Twitter and Reddit, mainly relying on tf-idf and keyword matching. Through a series of progressive refinements, we show the benefits of our approach through a simple qualitative analysis. Finally, results of a trial annotation experiment provide further support for the proposed method.

Contributions We summarise our contributions as follows:

1. a bottom-up approach to collect potential abusive and hateful messages on Twitter by using keywords based on controversial topics emerging from a different social media platform, Reddit, rather than manually selected by developers;
2. promote the cross-fertilisation of different language domains (i.e., Twitter and Reddit), facilitate the identification of implicit forms of abusive language or hate speech, and reduce top-down bias by avoiding preselection of keywords by dataset creators;
3. work towards the development of a reference corpus for Dutch annotated for abusive language and hate speech.

2. A Possible Solution

Finding instances of abusive or hateful messages in Social Media is not an easy task. Founta et al. (2018) has estimated that abusive messages represent between 0.1% and 3% (at most) of the messages in Twitter. Furthermore, one of our goals is to propose a methodology to improve the collection of potentially abusive messages across Social Media platforms, independently from their specific characteristics. For instance, the community-based approach can be easily applied on Social Media such as Facebook or Reddit since Facebook pages and sub-reddits can be interpreted as proxies for communities of users that share the same interests. However, such an approach cannot be applied on Twitter where such an aggregation of users is not possible given the peculiar structure of the platform.

Previous work (Graumans et al., 2019), however, has shown that controversies can actually be used as a viable proxy to collect and aggregate abusive language from Social Media, especially Twitter. Indeed, controversies are interactions among individuals or groups where the opinions of the involved parties do not change and tend to become more and more polarised towards extreme values (Timmermans et al., 2017). Such a dynamic of interactions and their polarised nature is a potential growth medium for abusive language and hate speech. A further advantage of using controversies to collect data is the reduction of topic bias factors. Although the proposed method will still use keywords to identify the data, such keywords have not been manually selected by the developers of the datasets but they are learned in a bottom-up approach from data that are perceived by the public at large or Social Media communities as divisive and potentially subject to a more extreme style of expression.

We focus on Twitter data rather than other Social Media platforms for a number of reasons, among which the most relevant are: (1.) possibility of (re-)distributing the data to the public, in compliance with the platform's terms of use and EU GDPR regulations; (2.) popularity of the platform in previous work on abusive language and hate speech, thus facilitating comparisons across languages and the development of cross-lingual models; (3.) ease of access to the data.

2.1. Method Overview

We conducted two initial experiments that could allow the identification of controversial topics on Twitter and thus extract potential abusive and hateful messages. The unfiltered Twitter dataset contains all public Dutch tweets posted in August 2018, corresponding to 14,122,350 tweets.

Twitter-based hashtag filter As an initial exploratory experiment, we tested whether using the N most frequent hashtags over a period of time could be a viable solution. The working hypothesis being: the more frequent the hashtag, the more likely it may refer to a controversy. We set the time frame to 1 month (i.e., August 2018), identified the most frequent hashtags (not necessarily corresponding to the trending topics in the targeted time span) and collected all tweets that contained them. The approach was quite a failure, as we mainly extracted tweets generated by bots and by account of professional institutions (e.g. news outlets), rather than actual users. We immediately dismissed this approach.

Reddit-based bag-of-words filter. This second experiment adopts a more refined approach and contextually investigates *cross-information* of Social Media platforms. We turned our attention on Reddit, a social media platform organised around specific channels ('subreddits'), using its filtering tools. Reddit allows its users to upvote and downvote posts, which resolves in a democratic procedure to give topics that deserve more attention precedence over topics considered less important. The tools can filter on top posts, thus showing the posts with the most upvotes, as well as on the so-called "controversial" posts, showing posts with a more or less equal amount of upvotes and downvotes. This is basically showing that the opinions on the relevance of the posts are mixed. We then retrieved two datasets: one of which was filtered on top posts (**top**), and another which was filtered on controversial posts (**controversial**), with no time restriction (i.e. use of the "all time" option). The top dataset contains 48 posts (for a total of 279,057 words) while the controversial dataset, contains 20 submissions (with a total of 23,794 words). All posts were taken from `r/thenetherlands`, a subreddit with 237,000 subscribers at the time of this study and with mainly Dutch contributions.

We then extracted unigram keywords per dataset using TF-IDF. In particular, we calculated TF-IDF over the union of the two datasets, i.e., **top** ∪ **controversial**, then we selected the k most important unigrams relative to each dataset, and retained only those of the controversial one. This procedure represents the core aspect of our bottom-up approach to select relevant keywords for highly controversial topics.

We then applied the controversial keywords to filter the 14M Twitter dataset extracting all messages that contain at least one of them. Next to this procedure, we also implemented a secondary filter based on the hashtags of all the extracted messages. We applied these additional set of hashtag-based keywords to retrieve additional messages from the 14M Twitter dataset. A visualization of the process is shown in Figure 1.

The final amount of collected messages by applying the two sets of keywords is 784,000 tweets (corresponding to 5.6% of the original 14M messages). A manual exploration of a portion of the new dataset has shown that the messages were actually referring to controversial topics and their origin was mainly from actual users rather than bots or by accounts of institutions.

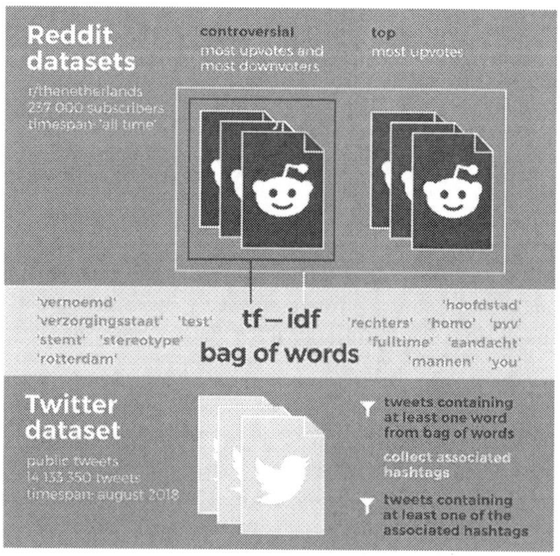

Figure 1: Reddit-based filtering process

3. Validation

After concluding that our second attempt seemed promising enough, we conducted a validation step to verify whether the filtering renders a higher density of tweets with abusive or hate speech instances. In addition, we also wanted to verify whether the filtered dataset potentially contained more interesting tweets for the abusive language and hate speech detection tasks. For the density aspect, we conducted a double annotation over a small random selection of 500 tweets from the filtered dataset and 500 tweets from the unfiltered one (Section 3.1.). For the qualitative aspect, we simply created word clouds of the two different sets of tweets, and observed which token would stand out most (Section 3.2.). This would give a rough but immediate idea of the most present topics in the two sets.

3.1. Annotation

We annotated the data by using a simplified version of the guidelines for hate speech annotation developed by Sanguinetti et al. (2018). We only considered the annotation parameter of hate speech [yes/no]. A tweet that would be annotated as containing hate speech should have a clear target of a minority group and should be "spreading, inciting, promoting or justifying hatred or violence toward the target, or aiming at dehumanizing, delegitimating, hurting or intimidating the target", as taken from the guidelines of (Sanguinetti et al., 2018).

To give some examples of tweets from the filtered dataset that were perceived as challenging to annotate:

1. Iedere scholier die toch een telefoon bij zich heeft/gebruikt op school krijgt 10 zweepslagen en meer bij recidivering. Maar dat zal wel niet mogen van die slappe homo's van @groenlinks @d66 hollandsezaken
   Every student carrying/using a mobile phone at school receives 10 whiplashes or more in case of recurrence. But the whimpy fags from @groenlinks @d66 probably won't allow that. hollandsezaken

2. RT @hulswood: Moskee-organisatie NL neemt Turkse jongeren mee op trainingkamp radicale imam: "trouw met zesjarig kind, mannen mogen vrouwen slaan, en steun gewapende jihad Syrië". ....was te verwachten, dit is islam. NL moet islamisering actief stoppen!
   RT @hulswood: Dutch mosque organization takes Turkish youth to training camp of radical imam: "marry a six year old, men are allowed to beat women, support the armed jihad in Syria". ... this was to be expected, this is Islam. The Netherlands has to actively stop islamization!

3. Schandalig om een hond met deze hitte aan een boom vast te binden. Doe je toch ook met pvv'ers niet?
   It is scandalous to tie a dog to a tree in this heat. You woudn't do that with a politician from the PVV either, right?

Though still low, a higher proportion of hate speech tweets was found in the filtered dataset. In Table 1 we show the confusion matrix for the two annotators over the two sets. After discussion and reconciliation, the total number of hateful tweets was 7 for the unfiltered dataset and 18 for the filtered one. There is a margin of disagreement that suggests further annotation is necessary, and for the moment led to interesting findings, also regarding the annotation guidelines.

Figure 2: Word cloud of unfiltered dataset (125 words are shown)

Figure 3: Word cloud of filtered dataset (125 words are shown)

Non filtered dataset		
	a1: 'no'	a1: 'yes'
a2: 'no'	491	1
a2: 'yes'	7	1

Filtered dataset		
	a1: 'no'	a1: 'yes'
a2: 'no'	464	4
a2: 'yes'	24	8

Table 1: Annotation confusion matrices for both datasets (before discussion and reconciliation).

The discussion over disagreements between the annotators showed an extra parameter that could possibly be taken into account (next to target and action) for the annotation guidelines, namely goal, that can be seen both as writer's intentions and message's effect on receivers. One annotator pointed out how for certain tweets no actual hate speech was expressed, e.g. the action of "spreading, inciting, promoting or justifying hatred or violence toward the target, or aiming at dehumanizing, delegitimating, hurting or intimidating", though the intentions of the user and the effects of the message could be interpreted as doing so. On the other hand, the other annotator had marked such tweets as non hate speech.
To clarify this issue consider the following example:

4. RT @SamvanRooy1: Qua symboliek kan dit tellen: in het Nederlandse Deventer verdwijnt een synagoge door toedoen van de gemeente en een Turkse ondernemer. Moslims erin, Joden eruit: bij gelijkblijvend beleid is dat het West-Europa van de toekomst. Video. islamisering
RT @SamvanRooy1: Symbolically this could count: a synagogue is taken out of service in the Dutch city

Deventer, because of the municipality and a Turkish businessman. Muslims in, Jews out: if this policy remains is this what West-Europe of the future looks like. Video. islamization

As Twitter is already using a hate speech filter, the tweets that are easier to track down are possibly already filtered out. For example, tweets with curses or death threats were not found. Tweets with less explicit, but more suggestive or subtle abusive language is left. Whether or not one can go as far to proclaim these to be hate speech is a challenging judgement, which could benefit from more elaborate and/or precise annotation guidelines. For instance, one useful distinction could be to annotate the explicitness of messages against a target rather than having a binary hate speech distinction (Waseem et al., 2017).

3.2. Topics

In Figure 2 and in Figure 3 we show the word clouds for the unfiltered and filtered datasets, respectively (125 words each). Any comment we can make about the two clouds is simply qualitative and should require a more structured analysis and further annotation.

At first sight, we can observe that in the filtered set, several of the words can indeed be signalling controversial topics. Examples are political parties (pvv, d66), politicians such as Wilders (wilders) (Dutch far-right politicians) and Rutte (rutte) (prime minister), morokkan (Moroccan), islam (Islam), feministen. The unfiltered set does not lend itself equally easily to meaningful clusters, showing quite generic, neutral terms such as echt (true) and genoeg (enough). Another quite clear example of this contrast between more specific *vs.* more generic in the two sets is provided by 'people' terms: the unfiltered set shows mensen ('people') and kinderen ('children'), while in the filtered set we find quite dominantly the terms for 'men' (mannen) and 'women' (vrouwen).

Some other terms can possibly be interpreted in connection with the time the Tweets were collected (August 2018), but with some degree of speculation. During that period, Amsterdam hosted the gay pride, which could have been the object of controversial comments. Rotterdam could be connected to the Rotterdam Rave Festival. Both sets show a reference to politie (police) that would require further analysis for proper understanding.

4. Future Directions

The recipe we have proposed here to maximise annotation effort over a meaningful and denser dataset for detecting abusive language, and to contextually minimise data selection bias, is only in its first experimental tests. However, we believe our results are promising and deserve further investigation, especially since this methodology could be applied to any language for which one can obtain Twitter and (controversial) Reddit data.

First, we need to annotate more data to confirm that the filtered dataset has indeed both a higher concentration of abusive language as well as overall a more interesting semantic profile, which ensures a more focused and challenging task. This need is also prompted by some discrepancy between the annotators; this is standardly observed in hate speech annotation, but we need to better understand whether filtering (or not) affects disagreement, and in which way. Second, we want to further explore and understand the potential of cross-fertilisation between different social media platform. This would also imply singling out and assessing the actual contribution of this aspect within our proposed recipe. Would it also be possible to use yet other platforms? Could we induce the filtering keywords through other channels maintaining our bottom-up strategy? Lastly, but importantly, we need to assess the actual quality of the filtered *vs.* unfiltered datasets in terms of training data for abusive language detection. Are we indeed creating 'better' data for predictive models? For a proper test of this sort, the test data would need to be acquired independently of our suggested strategy, which however could incur the classic problem of top-down bias which we wanted to avoid in the first place. This test clearly requires proper modelling, possibly under different settings.

5. Acknolwedgement

We would like to thank Arjan Schelhaas for contributing to the annotation, and the anonymous reviewers for their helpful comments.

6. Bibliographical References

Basile, V., Bosco, C., Fersini, E., Nozza, D., Patti, V., Rangel Pardo, F. M., Rosso, P., and Sanguinetti, M. (2019). SemEval-2019 task 5: Multilingual detection of hate speech against immigrants and women in twitter. In *Proceedings of the 13th International Workshop on Semantic Evaluation*, pages 54–63, Minneapolis, Minnesota, USA, June. Association for Computational Linguistics.

Bosco, C., Dell'Orletta, Felice, F. P., Sanguinetti, M., and Tesconi, M. (2018). Overview of the EVALITA Hate Speech Detection (HaSpeeDe) Task. In Tommaso Caselli, et al., editors, *Proceedings of the 6th evaluation campaign of Natural Language Processing and Speech tools for Italian (EVALITA'18)*, Turin, Italy. CEUR.org.

Fersini, E., Rosso, P., and Anzovino, M. (2018). Overview of the task on automatic misogyny identification at ibereval 2018. In *IberEval@SEPLN.*

Founta, A. M., Djouvas, C., Chatzakou, D., Leontiadis, I., Blackburn, J., Stringhini, G., Vakali, A., Sirivianos, M., and Kourtellis, N. (2018). Large scale crowdsourcing and characterization of twitter abusive behavior. In *Twelfth International AAAI Conference on Web and Social Media.*

Graumans, L., David, R., and Caselli, T. (2019). Twitter-based polarised embeddings for abusive language detection. In *2019 8th International Conference on Affective Computing and Intelligent Interaction Workshops and Demos (ACIIW)*. IEEE, 9.

Jurgens, D., Hemphill, L., and Chandrasekharan, E. (2019). A just and comprehensive strategy for using NLP to address online abuse. In *Proceedings of the 57th Annual Meeting of the Association for Computational Linguistics*, pages 3658–3666, Florence, Italy, July. Association for Computational Linguistics.

Merenda, F., Zaghi, C., Caselli, T., and Nissim, M. (2018). Source-driven Representations for Hate Speech Detection, proceedings of the 5th italian conference on computational linguistics (clic-it 2018). Turin, Italy.

Ribeiro, M. H., Calais, P. H., Santos, Y. A., Almeida, V. A., and Meira Jr, W. (2018). Characterizing and detecting hateful users on twitter. In *Twelfth International AAAI Conference on Web and Social Media*.

Sanguinetti, M., Poletto, F., Bosco, C., Patti, V., and Stranisci, M. (2018). An Italian Twitter Corpus of Hate Speech against Immigrants. In Nicoletta Calzolari (Conference chair), et al., editors, *Proceedings of the Eleventh International Conference on Language Resources and Evaluation (LREC 2018)*, Miyazaki, Japan, May 7-12, 2018. European Language Resources Association (ELRA).

Timmermans, B., Aroyo, L., Tobias Kuhn, Kaspar Beelen, E. K., and Bob van de Velde, G. v. E. (2017). Controcurator: Understanding controversy using collective intelligence. In *Collective Intelligence 2017*.

Tulkens, S., Hilte, L., Lodewyckx, E., Verhoeven, B., and Daelemans, W. (2016). A dictionary-based approach to racism detection in dutch social media. In *Proceedings of the first Workshop on Text Analytics for Cybersecurity and Online Safety (TA-COS 2016)/Daelemans, Walter [edit.]; et al.*, pages 1–7.

Vidgen, B., Harris, A., Nguyen, D., Tromble, R., Hale, S., and Margetts, H. (2019). Challenges and frontiers in abusive content detection. In *Proceedings of the Third Workshop on Abusive Language Online*, pages 80–93, Florence, Italy, August. Association for Computational Linguistics.

Waseem, Z. and Hovy, D. (2016). Hateful symbols or hateful people? predictive features for hate speech detection on twitter. In *Proceedings of the NAACL student research workshop*, pages 88–93.

Waseem, Z., Davidson, T., Warmsley, D., and Weber, I. (2017). Understanding abuse: A typology of abusive language detection subtasks. In *Proceedings of the First Workshop on Abusive Language Online*, pages 78–84.

Wiegand, M., Ruppenhofer, J., Schmidt, A., and Greenberg, C. (2018). Inducing a lexicon of abusive words–a feature-based approach. In *Proceedings of the 2018 Conference of the North American Chapter of the Association for Computational Linguistics: Human Language Technologies, Volume 1 (Long Papers)*, pages 1046–1056.

Wiegand, M., Ruppenhofer, J., and Kleinbauer, T. (2019). Detection of Abusive Language: the Problem of Biased Datasets. In *Proceedings of the 2019 Conference of the North American Chapter of the Association for Computational Linguistics: Human Language Technologies, Volume 1 (Long and Short Papers)*, pages 602–608, Minneapolis, Minnesota, June. Association for Computational Linguistics.

Zampieri, M., Malmasi, S., Nakov, P., Rosenthal, S., Farra, N., and Kumar, R. (2019a). Predicting the Type and Target of Offensive Posts in Social Media. In *Proceedings of NAACL*.

Zampieri, M., Malmasi, S., Nakov, P., Rosenthal, S., Farra, N., and Kumar, R. (2019b). SemEval-2019 task 6: Identifying and categorizing offensive language in social media (OffensEval). In *Proceedings of the 13th International Workshop on Semantic Evaluation*, pages 75–86, Minneapolis, Minnesota, USA, June. Association for Computational Linguistics.

Association for Computational Linguistics
209 N. Eighth Street
Stroudsburg, Pennsylvania 18360

ISBN 978-1-7138-1276-0

CURRAN ASSOCIATES INC.
proceedings.com